ousand eyes were on him
is hands with dirt;
housand tongues applau
iped them on his shirt.
while the writhing pitcher
nto his hip,
ce gleamed in Casey's eye
asey's lip.

now the leather-covered
urtling through the air,
Casey stood a-watching
randeur there.

CASEY AT THE BAT

Special thanks to: Rick Swig, for loaning Willard Mullin's
original "Casey" artwork; Jason Powers, for hand-painting
Mullin's original pen and ink drawings for this edition; and
Jeff Spingeld, for research assistance.

Editor: Michael Powers
Editorial Supervisor and Associate Publisher: Eric Reynolds
Book Design: Keeli McCarthy
Production: Jason Powers and Paul Baresh
Publisher: Gary Groth

FANTAGRAPHICS BOOKS, INC.
7563 Lake City Way NE
Seattle, Washington, 98115

ISBN 978-1-60699-814-4

First printing: April, 2015
Printed in Malaysia

Library of Congress Control Number: 2014954771

Willard Mullin's Casey at the Bat

And Other Diamond Tales

With Ernest Thayer
Foreword by Yogi Berra

FANTAGRAPHICS BOOKS

New York Yankees rookie Yogi Berra shakes hands with the retired "Sultan of Swat," Babe Ruth, in 1947.

Foreword

Baseball and newspapers used to go together like hand and glove. That's what we lived on to get all the game stories and results, to see who was hot, and who wasn't. It's different today with the Internet and *SportsCenter* and so much media. But when I played in New York in the '50s, there were eight daily newspapers, and we read almost all of 'em.

I always liked the *New York World Telegram* because they had something nobody else had — the best cartoonist. I only met Willard Mullin a couple of times, but everyone knew his work. His drawings of players and teams were dandy — so were his comments.

I didn't mind when he drew me — he did me pretty good. In my rookie year, 1947, he compared me on the cover of *The Sporting News* to my boyhood idol, Joe Medwick, as a bad-ball hitter. Once he poked fun at my contract-haggling with the Yankees, showing me talking in some kind of royal English. "I am unable to reconcile the triviality of the engendered lagniappe to the quality of services rendered . . . "

It was amusing. I enjoyed seeing Mullin's cartoons on the front page of *The Sporting News*, the baseball bible. He captured the fun and specialness of the game. Sometimes he'd be funny, sometimes sentimental. Mullin's cartoons were always sharp. He connected to the fans because he was one. And everyone I knew was a fan of his.

—YOGI BERRA

Willard
and Casey

"I'm not an artist, I'm a cartoonist." —Willard Mullin

"That ain't my style, said Casey" —Ernest Lawrence Thayer

The Mighty Casey, the archetypal slugger, has fascinated artists in every medium for the century and a quarter since his birth in 1888. On June 3rd of that year, Ernest Lawrence Thayer published "Casey at the Bat" in his humor column in the *San Francisco Examiner*. While not an immediate hit, Casey caught on in part due to the dramatic recitations of DeWolf Hopper, an accomplished actor for whom "Casey" became his signature piece. Since then, Casey has appeared in paintings and sculpture, in prose, poetry, fiction, essays, comedy routines, pop songs, comic books, movies, cartoons, even an opera and a ballet. Casey has even been a shaving mug sold with aftershave by Avon! "Casey at the Bat," while not the first piece of baseball literature, surely casts the longest shadow of any piece written about the sport.

T.S. Eliot paid homage in "Growltiger's Last Stand." The Eagles mentioned him in "Rocky Mountain Way," and John Fogerty name-checked him in "Centerfield." Death Cab For Cutie has a song entitled "No Joy In Mudville." Casey has been referenced in songs by Josh Ritter and Blues Traveler. He's been recited by everyone from Vin Scully to Tug McGraw to Vincent Price. Garrison Keillor does a hilarious piece from the other team's perspective, "Casey at the Bat (Road Game)." William Schuman wrote an opera about him, and there is also a ballet choreographed by Lisa de Ribere.

Every time something significant happens in baseball, and often in politics or other arenas, there is a parody written: "Obama" or "Palin at the Bat" (you could look it up, as another famous Casey once said, and I encourage you to do so). A brief scan through the Baseball Hall of Fame library's file of Casey parodies finds everyone from Ben Bernanke to Bud Selig getting the treatment—and for ballplayers, everyone from Home Run Baker to Enos Slaughter to Derek Jeter has been cast in the role of updated Casey. Sometimes Casey gets to play the hero, as when the poem is used to tell the stories of Bobby Thomson, Don Larsen, Jackie Robinson, or Bucky Dent. Even both sides of the Microsoft vs. Apple debate have weighed in with parodies called "Gatesy at the Bat," and "Steven Saves the Mac."

Ray Bradbury reset his tale within the world of *Moby-Dick* in "Ahab at the Helm." ("It looked extremely rocky for the Melville Nine that day . . .") Frank Jacobs rewrote the poem as if it had been written by Edgar Allan Poe. ("Once upon a final inning, with the other ball team winning...") The Mighty Casey's epic tale has been made into a movie several times, beginning with an Edison feature in 1899. Wallace Beery played Casey in 1927, and other silents and shorts on the Casey theme were made in 1913, 1916, and 1976.

Casey got the Disney animation treatment twice, with a straight version in 1946, and a 1954 version in which Casey manages the Caseyettes—a team made up of his nine daughters. Grantland Rice, H.I. Phillips, Foster Brooks and others wrote frequent updates to the poem such as "Casey's Revenge," "Casey—Twenty Years Later," and "Mighty Casey's Ghost." Lesser poets have sent Casey's son, grandson, daughter, wife, sister, mother, and aunt up to the plate in attempts to clear the family name. He even has his own episodes of *The Twilight Zone* and *Northern Exposure*.

Visual artists have been taking a crack at Casey from almost the very beginning. Children's book versions have been published by more than a dozen artists and illustrators, including Gerald Fitzgerald, Barry Moser, Christopher Bing, Patricia Polacco, and LeRoy Neiman.

Every baseball artist does Casey. None has done him quite like Willard Mullin, for Casey, of course, is a bum. Mullin, the longtime newspaper sports cartoonist, is best known for creating the Brooklyn Bum, the affable symbol of the Brooklyn Dodgers—a fine fellow who just can't get it done, but whom we love anyway—a latter day Casey, in a way.

After a few years in the bush leagues, Mullin hit The Big Apple in 1934, when he began drawing for the *New York World-Telegram*. If you read baseball coverage in the 20th century, you know his widely repeated work, which was frequently featured in *The Sporting News*, *Time*, *Life*, and *The Saturday Evening Post*.

Mullin was honored with the Sports Cartoonists Award from the National Cartoonists Society eight times, from 1957-62, and again in 1964-65. He won the Reuben, the organization's highest honor, given to the "outstanding cartoonist of the year," in 1954. The next year it was won for the first time by Charles Schulz, who mentioned Mullin in a later *Peanuts* strip. Lucy was angry that she'd hurt her arm playing baseball, and threatened to sue Abner Doubleday, Babe Ruth, and Willard Mullin. Upon his retirement in 1971, the organization named Mullin "Sports Cartoonist of the 20th Century."
Sportswriter Dan Daniel called him "The greatest stylist of his profession," and Red Smith wrote "there never was another who combined such news sense and wit and perception with such a comic pen."

Mullin drew his take on "Casey at the Bat" for the National Association's fiftieth anniversary in 1951. The NA was the umbrella organization for minor league baseball. Mullin drew thirteen views of The Mighty Casey, to correspond to the poem's thirteen verses. Each verse and corresponding drawing was featured on a separate juice glass. The glasses could only be purchased by minor league baseball teams, for use as promotional items. In a flyer advertising the glasses to member teams, the NA suggests that they be given away one at a time: "They lend themselves to a continuous promotion of Ladies Day, for example, if you care to give away one glass each Ladies Day until your patrons have acquired a full set and naturally the full poem." The flyer called Mullin "the king of cartoon humor."

While the glasses were meant to retail in the 25-cent range if sold, rather than given away, they command a much higher price today. Full sets, which rarely surface on eBay, can go for around a hundred dollars. If you are like me, you have a set that is missing just one or two glasses.

Who is Casey, and why does his tale—a tale of failure, after all— continue to fascinate us well more than a century later? Casey, of course, is us. He is the accumulation, the apotheosis of our hopes and dreams, not just for our baseball teams, but for our selves, and for our lives. And his hometown team, the Mudville Nine, is also us. Mudville is our home—never quite Yankee Stadium or the White House or Hollywood, but a place of dreams nonetheless. Just as Casey is Everyman, Mudville is everybody's hometown. One of my sidelines for the last sixteen years has been "being Casey," dressing up in a late 19th-century style uniform and acting out the poem to groups ranging from school kids to Baseball Hall of Fame induction ceremony audiences. Over those years, I have performed the poem perhaps two thousand times—I never kept count, but that's a decent estimate. Sharing this poem with this many audiences, often followed by Q and A sessions, has given me many insights into why we love this poem and its protagonist. To begin with, Casey runs against the grain of storytelling. His expected happy ending never happens, and instead, we are left just as he is, failed, powerless, sad, tragic, and alone. To paraphrase the great broadcaster Ernie Harwell, Casey "just stood there

like a house by the side of the road," at least for the first two strikes. One of baseball's genius components is the game's dramatic structure, which allows for a cliff-hanging ending at any point—time is irrelevant as there is no game clock and so hope is always alive, and improbable comebacks occur with regularity.

And probable comebacks occur as well. Our favorite players get the big hit with two outs and the game on the line, don't they? Fairly often. Surely with The Mighty Casey up there doing our bidding, we are likely to put this one in the win column, right? Oh if Casey could just get hold of one here—we are on the edge of our seats, basking in the perfect drama that is baseball. And, though it was written so long ago, no subsequent work of baseball literature has ever done a better job of representing baseball's stark game of wins and losses. The confrontation between the batter and the pitcher is epic, naked, elemental. I once mentioned to an elderly male friend, a WWII military pilot, that I thought this confrontation was the most starkly challenging moment in sports. He disagreed, saying that I was only half right—it was the most existential moment in life itself.

The game is on the line. And who should come to the plate but Casey, The Mighty Casey, our cleanup man. The best hitter we have. Winner of many ball games past. Casey looks at a first strike—not his style. He takes another one, perhaps on purpose, to set up and cue up his upcoming triumph. With Casey we cannot fail. Here's the pitch . . .

—Tim Wiles

Casey at the Bat

By
Ernest Thayer

Illustrations
By
Willard Mullin

1

It looked extremely rocky
  for the Mudville nine that day,
The score stood four to six
  with but an inning left to play.
And so when Cooney died at first,
  and Burrows did the same,
A pallor wreathed the features
  of the patrons of the game.

2

3

A straggling few got up to go,
  leaving there the rest,
With the hope that springs eternal
  within the human breast.
For they thought if only Casey
  could but get a whack at that,
They'd put up even money
  with Casey at the bat!

4

5

But Flynn preceded Casey,
  and likewise so did Blake,
And the former was a pudding
  and the latter was a fake;
So on the stricken multitude
  a death-like silence sat,
For there seemed but little chance
  of Casey's getting to the bat.

7

But Flynn let drive a single
  to the wonderment of all,
And the much despised Blakey
  tore the cover off the ball,
And when the dust had lifted
  and they saw what had occurred
There was Blakey safe at second,
  and Flynn a-hugging third.

8

9

Then from the gladdened multitude
  went up a joyous yell,
It bounded from the mountain top
  and rattled in the dell,
It struck upon the hillside
  and rebounded on the flat,
For Casey, mighty Casey,
  was advancing to the bat.

11

There was ease in Casey's manner
   as he stepped into his place,
There was pride in Casey's bearing
   and a smile on Casey's face,
And when responding to the cheers
   he lightly doffed his hat,
No stranger in the crowd could doubt,
   'twas Casey at the bat.

13

Ten thousand eyes were on him
  as he rubbed his hands with dirt,
Five thousand tongues applauded
  as he wiped them on his shirt;
And while the writhing pitcher
  ground the ball into his hip—
Defiance gleamed in Casey's eye—
  a sneer curled Casey's lip.

14

15

And now the leather-covered sphere
came hurtling through the air,
And Casey stood a-watching it
in haughty grandeur there;
Close by the sturdy batsman
the ball unheeded sped-
"That hain't my style," said Casey-
"Strike one," the umpire said.

17

From the bleachers black with people
there rose a sullen roar,
Like the beating of the storm waves
on a stern and distant shore,
"Kill him! kill the Umpire!"
shouted someone from the stand—
And it's likely they'd have done it
had not Casey raised his hand.

19

With a smile of Christian charity
  great Casey's visage shone,
He stilled the rising tumult
  and he bade the game go on;
He signaled to the pitcher
  and again the spheroid flew,
But Casey still ignored it
  and the Umpire said, "Strike two."

21

"Fraud!" yelled the maddened thousands,
  and echo answered "Fraud,"
But one scornful look from Casey
  and the audience was awed;
They saw his face grow stern and cold,
  they saw his muscles. strain
And they knew that Casey
  would not let that ball go by again.

22

23

The sneer is gone from Casey's lip;
  his teeth are clenched with hate,
He pounds with cruel violence
  his bat upon the plate;
And now the pitcher holds the ball,
  and now he lets it go,
And now the air is shattered
  by the force of Casey's blow.

25

Oh! somewhere in this favored land
 the sun is shining bright,
The band is playing somewhere,
 and somewhere hearts are light,
And somewhere men are laughing,
 and somewhere children shout;
But there is no joy in Mudville—
 mighty Casey has **STRUCK OUT!**

The Longfellow of
the Sports
Page

During his lifetime, Willard Mullin was frequently referred to as "The Rembrandt of the Sports Page," but perhaps his sobriquet should have also included "The Longfellow of the Sports Page." Mullin's contribution to baseball's lexicon is without equal. He was responsible for giving Lou Gehrig his nickname "The Iron Horse." He gave the '34 Cardinals their nickname, "The Gashouse Gang." He referred to the World Series between the NY Giants and the NY Yankees in 1936 as the "Subway Series" (a moniker that has been used to describe every World Series between New York-based teams since). And, of course, there was his most famous creation: the "Brooklyn Bum."

In 1951, Mullin was responsible for characterizing the Giants' run to the pennant as the "Miracle of Coogan's Bluff" and Bobby Thomson's climatic homerun as "The Shot Heard 'Round the World." It is in his poetry, however, where it becomes truly evident that Mullin's artistry encompassed more than just cartooning.

His poem "Iron Horse Lou" [fig. 1] is still published every year on the anniversary of Lou Gehrig's famous "Luckiest Man on the Face of this Earth" speech (July 4th, 1939). It was, however, actually first published in the *New York World Telegram* on May 3, 1939, the day after Gehrig's legendary streak ended at 2,130 games.

This poem not only illustrates Mullin's way with a poetic phrase, it also draws on Willard's deep knowledge and understanding of 18th and 19th century American poetry. "Iron Horse Lou" is based on Oliver Wendell Holmes' "The Deacon's Masterpiece *or* the Wonderful One Horse Shay." In that poem, the shay was constructed from the very best of materials so that each part was as strong as every other part. The shay endures for 100 years and then it *went to pieces all at once and nothing first / just as bubbles do when they burst*. What an appropriate metaphor for the life and career of Lou Gehrig.

Mullin's parody of Longfellow's "The Village Blacksmith" [fig. 2] appropriately accompanies his drawing of Lou Gehrig's contract negotiations with the Yankees in the winter of 1936–37. Also during the '30s, when the Dodgers were frequently awful, Mullin penned an untitled and unpublished poem written on his personal letterhead [fig. 3]. It has a Brooklyn fan, speaking pure Brooklynese, as only Mullin could write it, appearing before a judge after having assaulted a Giants fan earlier in the day at Ebbets Field, for giving him the "business." Mullin even references a famous incident in Dodgers lore: when the legendary Babe Herman had hit into a triple play, the result of all three runners ending up at third base at the same time!

In 1949, after the Yankees had beaten the Brooklyn Dodgers yet again in the World Series, Willard penned the parody of Walt Whitman's "O Captain, My Captain" entitled "Brooklyn, My Brooklyn" [fig. 4] to articulate the despair of the Dodger faithful.

Mullin's lettering was truly distinctive and almost as famous as his drawings, the quintessential example being his iconic signature which consisted of 25 vertical lines and one horizontal. 1953 saw Ol' Will create his baseball alphabet, "From April to Zeptember" [fig. 5], making sure to include "D is for Dodger . . . G is for Giants . . . [and] Y is for Yankees" before concluding with "Z is for . . . darned if we know . . . (We're in a helluva fix)."

In 1951, Mullin once again exhibited his knowledge of American poetry with his parody of James T. Fields' "The Owl Critic" [fig. 6], which had as its chorus "And the Barber Kept Shaving" to illustrate so appropriately the contribution Sal "the Barber" Maglie made to the Giants pennant-winning season.

Mullin's final literary contribution came on September 5, 1969, when his cover drawing for *Time* magazine included "Go-Go" behind the image of the Mets [fig. 7], thus giving them their famous nickname, "the Go-Go Mets."

At the time of Mullin's retirement, Red Smith, the Pulitzer Prize-winning sportswriter and Mullin's good friend, confessed, "I have lost track of the number of ideas for columns I have stolen from Willard's drawings over the years."

Willard Mullin was a member of the Baseball Writers Association for over 35 years. Very rarely did Mullin ever create an image without some accompanying editorial comment. But despite all of this, Mullin has never been awarded or even nominated for the J.G. Taylor Spink Award, given by the BBWA "for meritorious contributions to baseball writing." Attempts to have him considered for this award, which is ironically named after one of his best friends, J.G. Taylor Spink, for whom Willard created over 250 covers for Spink's *Sporting News* alone, have been dismissed by current members of the Association as inappropriate because he "only drew cartoons."

It is hoped that this modest volume of Mullin's work will encourage the BBWA to reconsider their position and bestow on Willard Mullin the J.G. Taylor Spink Award he so richly deserves.

— *Michael Power.*

Iron Horse Lou

You've heard of the wonderful
Iron Horse Lou,
Who looked as if he would
never be through
For fourteen years as good
as new,
And then of a sudden, he —
ah, its true! —
I'll tell you what happened
without ado,
Scaring McCarthy into fits,
Frightening Yank fans out of
their wits, —
Did you ever think it could
happen to Lou?

Now in building a player,
I tell you what,
There is always *somewhere*
a weakest spot; —
In arm, foot, elbow, in thigh
or slat;
In body, or shoulder, or neck
or at bat,
In fielding, or hitting, or feet
that are flat,
Something someplace will fold
like a hat.

And thats the reason, beyond
a doubt,
That a player *breaks down*
but doesn't *wear out!*

But Gehrig was not like the
common folk;
Created, was he, like the
strongest oak;
Seemed nothing could crack
on this hardy bloke!

No flaw to be found, no
use to try
With hand as good and sure
as his eye,
His arm was just as strong
as his knee;
His back and shoulders enough
for three;
And his legs the best you
ever did see.

Tops! I tell you, I rather
guess
He was a wonder and nothing
less!

Players they came for a
year or two,
Stayed a while --- were re-
placed by new.
Dugan, Ruth, Meusel, all are
through
But there stood the stout, old
Iron Horse Lou
Playing the bag as the best
could do!

A thousand ball games
passed and found
Gehrig at first base strong
and sound.
Fifteen hundred came and
went;
Eighteen hundred - and still
unbent.
And then the two-thousand
twenty first game
Playing as usual, much the
same.

Piling a record gol-darn
purty,
Came two thousand one hundred
and thirty.

Nineteen thirtynine, the first
day of May —
About the Oak's temples the
hair had turned gray,
A general flavor of mild decay,
But nothing local as one
may say.

His body was sturdy - just like
at the start;
His lungs were still as strong
as his heart,
He was sound all over as any
part, —
And yet, as *a whole*, it is past
a doubt
In one more game he will
be *worn out!*

The second of May, Thirty
nine!
McCarthy was naming his
men down the line —

And what do you think the
people found?
Dahlgren on first to the right
of the mound!
And off in the dugout with
head going round
Was the man who had played
himself into the ground.

You see, of course, if you're
not a dunce
How he went to pieces all
at once, —
All at once, and nothing first, —
Just as bubbles do when
they burst.

End of the wonderful Iron
Horse Lou.
Flesh is flesh — and Lou is
through.

APOLOGIES TO OLIVER WENDELL HOLMES — AND HIS "THE DEACON'S MASTERPIECE"

fig. 1

fig 2

EV'RY TIME YA LOOKS UP
   WE GOT A NEW GUY OUT ON TH' HILL.

AN' IT WON'T BE TH' LAST O' TH' NINT'
   WE CAN'T GET A RUN UNTIL

THEN WE GETS A WALK AN' A SINGLE
   AN' TH' NEX' GUY GETS' HIT
      WIT' TH' BALL .
   SO I TOINED T' THIS SQUARE
   AN' I PERNTED OUT THERE
      AN' I SAYS," NOW WE GOT
      T'REE GUYS ON BASE!"

   AN' HE LEANT OVER,
   AN' I SWEAR T' YOU
   HE LAUGHED LIKE A HYENER
   IN PROSPEC' ZOO,
      AN' HE SAYS,
      "WHICH BASE?"
   THAT'S WHEN I LEFT HIM HAVE IT, JUDGE
      RIGHT IN TH' FACE!

THANKS F'R DISMISSIN' TH' CASE, JUDGE.
THANKS F'R TRUNIN' IT OUT.
   A GUY CAN'T STAN' ONLY SO MUCH,
   AN' OUR BUMS WUZ DEAD JUST ABOUT.

I'M OUT AT EBBETS
   WATCHIN' OUR BUMS DO THEH STUFF,
AN' SETTIN' RIGHT BACK OF ME
   IS THIS HEEL F'M COOGAN'S BLUFF,
AN' F'R EIGHT FULL INNINS, JUDGE
   I'M TAKIN' THIS WISE GUY'S GUFF.

      THE LUCK THEM BUMS HAVE
         I'M TELLIN' YA
      IS NUTTIN' BUT A SCANDAL.
         THEY SCRATCH ONE T'RUH
         THAT GOES F'R TUH
         AN' THEY GETS ONE OFF'N
         TH' HANDLE ——
AN' TH' NEX' ONES IN BEDF'D AVE-NUH.

THANKS AGAIN, Y'R HONOR,
   I KNOW'D Y'D UNNERSTAN'.
I COULD OF TOOK HIM
   AN' BEAT HIM UP UNNER TH' STAN',
BUT WE'RE ONLY TRAILIN' BY EIGHT NOW,
   WIT' ONLY TWO OUT IN TH' NINT'.
THAT AIN'T NO TIME T' TAKE OUT
   F'R A FIGHT, JUDGE!
   SEE YEZ AT EBBETS T'NIGHT

fig. 3

Brooklyn, My Brooklyn

O,Yankees! O,Yankees! your fearful trip is done,
Your ship has weather'd every rack, the pri
   sought is won.
     But O, DiMaggio! Henrich! Phil!
      From you has all pity fled?
       Look! on the deck my Brooklyn
       Fallen cold and dead.

Here, Brooklyn! dear Brooklyn!
   My arm beneath your head!
     It is some dream that on the deck
      You've fallen cold and dead.

The ship is anchor'd safe and sound, its voya
   closed and done,
From fearful trip the victor ship comes in wi
   object won;
     Exult O shores! and ring, O bells!
      But I with mournful tread
       Walk the deck my Brooklyn lies
       Fallen cold and dead.

fig 4

From April to Zeptember

fig 5

fig. 6

fig 7

The "Dean of Sports Cartooning," **WILLARD HARLAN MULLIN** (1902-1978), was born near Columbus, Ohio, but grew up in Los Angeles, California. He began his professional career as a cartoonist in 1923 working for the *Los Angeles Herald* first doing spot illustrations and later sports cartoons. He moved to New York in 1934 to become a sports cartoonist for the *New York World-Telegram*, where he created the infamous "Brooklyn Bum" character that became synonymous with the Brooklyn Dodgers. He also worked for the *The Saturday Evening Post*, *Time*, and *Life*. Comics historian Maurice Horn stated that "Mullin's love of his craft and of his subjects shone through in all of his cartoons: under the surface roughness lurked a strong undercurrent of affection and optimism." He greatly defined the modern sports cartoon, now a dying art form, by combining representative portraiture, cartooning, and editorial commentary.

Known as much for his "Yogi-isms" as his Hall of Fame catching abilities, **LAWRENCE PETER "YOGI" BERRA** played on ten World Series championship teams for the New York Yankees. Berra was selected to the All-Star team every year from 1948 to 1962 and was a three-time American League MVP. He caught three no-hitters, including Don Larsen's perfect game in the 1956 World Series.

MICHAEL POWERS is an attorney who has represented the Estate of Willard Mullin for over 15 years. During that time, he has located and catalogued over 3,000 Mullin images including all those contained in this volume. He curated the largest exhibit of Mullin's work, in 2003 at the Society of Illustrators in New York City, and the permanent Mullin exhibit at the San Francisco Giants' AT&T Park.

TIM WILES, Director of the Guilderland, NY Public Library, was Director of Research at the Baseball Hall of Fame Library from 1995-2014. He began performing Casey at the Bat in 1997, and has performed approximately 2,000 times since, for audiences in 22 states. He has written two other baseball books.

and distant shore.

Kill him! Kill the umpir
one on the stand;

d it's likely they'd have
Casey raised his hand.

ith a smile of Christian ch
visage shone;

stilled the rising tumult
go on;

signaled to the pitcher,
spheroid flew;

t Casey still ignored it, an
"Strike two."